A BOOK   FOR MY
Sister

PAMELA WINTERBOURNE

LAUGHING ELEPHANT   MMI

Far or near I think of you,

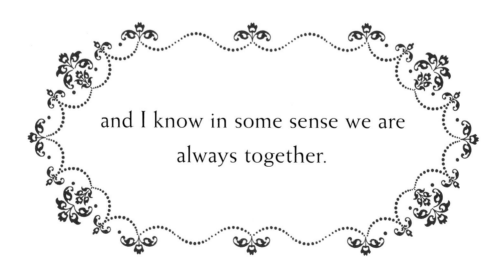

and I know in some sense we are
always together.

We have always been able
to share confidences.

We are made closer
by memories held in common.

We comfort each other
in times of sorrow,

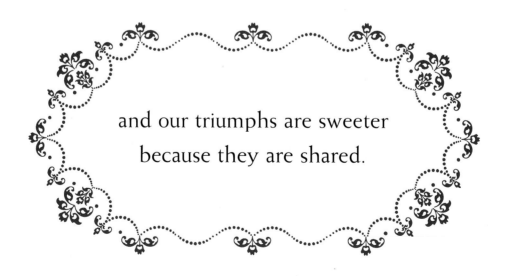

and our triumphs are sweeter
because they are shared.

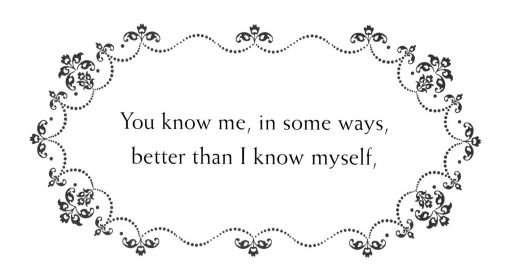

You know me, in some ways,
better than I know myself,

15

and we have both been
enriched by our various interests
and experiences.

We have grown
and learned together.

I remember much laughter shared.

I feel safe in your esteem,
which allows me to share
my dreams and aspirations.

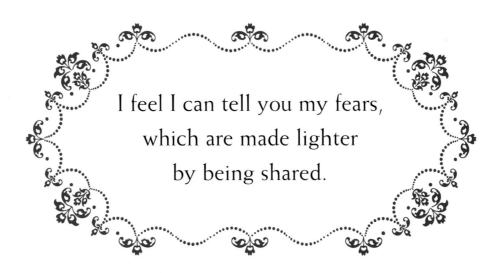

I feel I can tell you my fears,
which are made lighter
by being shared.

You are a mirror
in which I can see what I was,
and what I have become.

27

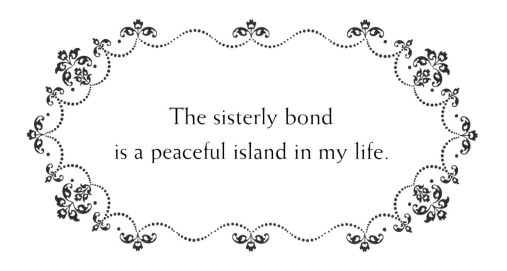

The sisterly bond
is a peaceful island in my life.

I delight in both our similarities
and our differences

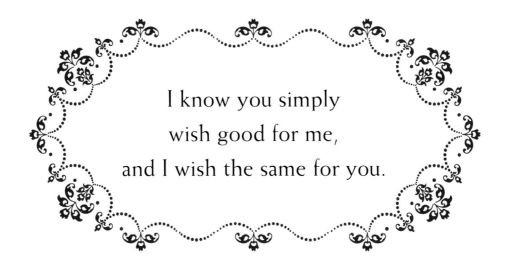

I know you simply
wish good for me,
and I wish the same for you.

33

PICTURE CREDITS